DATE DUE MAR 0 6

GAYLORD

TRIBES of NATIVE AMERICA

Chumash

edited by Marla Felkins Ryan
and Linda Schmittroth

BLACKBIRCH®
PRESS

THOMSON

GALE

For more information, contact
The Gale Group, Inc.
27500 Drake Rd.
Farmington Hills, MI 48331-3535
Or you can visit our Internet site at http://www.gale.com

Photo credits: Cover Courtesy of Northwestern University Library; cover © National Archives;
cover © Photospin; cover © Perry Jasper Photography; cover © Picturequest; cover © Seattle
Post-Intelligencer Collection, Museum of History & Industry; cover © PhotoDisc; cover © Library
of Congress; page 5 © Royalty-Free/Corbis; page 6 © Shelley Gazin/Corbis; page 7 © Channel
Islands National Marine Sanctuary; page 8 © Bowers Museum of Cultural Art/Corbis; pages 9,
26, 30 © Nik Wheeler/Corbis; pages 11, 12, 15, 17, 23, 24 © North Wind Picture Archives; pages
13, 14, 26 © David Muench/Corbis; page 18 © Robert Holmes/Corbis; page 20 © Corel; page 21
© Chuck Place/Chuck Place Photography; page 22 © Bancroft Library, UC Berkeley; page 25 ©
Henry Diltz/Corbis; page 28 © Pat O'Hara/Corbis; page 29 © Dennis di Cicco/Corbis; page 31 ©
historypictures.com

LIBRARY OF CONGRESS CATALOGING-IN-PUBLICATION DATA

Chumash / Marla Felkins Ryan, book editor ; Linda Schmittroth, book editor.
 v. cm. — (Tribes of Native America)
Includes bibliographical references and index.
Contents: Name — History — Government — Daily life — Current tribal issues.
 ISBN 1-56711-724-4 (alk. paper)
 1. Chumash Indians—History—Juvenile literature. 2. Chumash
Indians—Social life and customs—Juvenile literature. [1. Chumash
Indians. 2. Indians of North America—California.] I. Ryan, Marla
Felkins. II. Schmittroth, Linda. III. Series.

 E99.C815C48 2003
 979.4004'9757—dc21

                                                        2003002628

Printed in United States
10 9 8 7 6 5 4 3 2 1

Table of Contents

CHUMASH

Name

The name *Chumash* comes from a word the tribe called people who lived on one of the Santa Barbara Channel Islands. The Spanish called every group of Indians who lived on these islands and along the southern coast of California the *Chumash*.

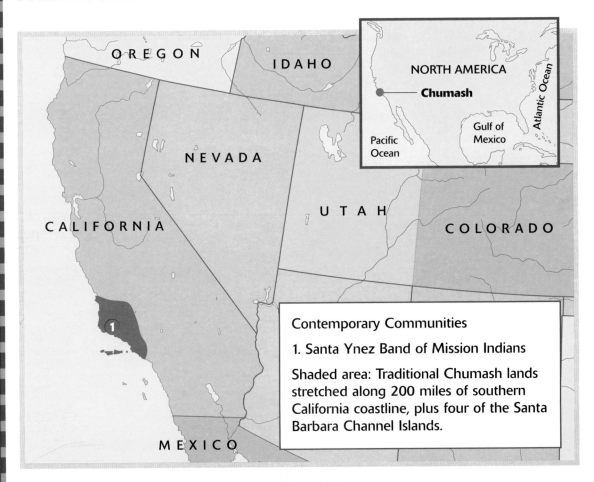

NORTH AMERICA

Chumash

Pacific Ocean

Gulf of Mexico

Atlantic Ocean

OREGON

IDAHO

NEVADA

UTAH

CALIFORNIA

COLORADO

MEXICO

Contemporary Communities

1. Santa Ynez Band of Mission Indians

Shaded area: Traditional Chumash lands stretched along 200 miles of southern California coastline, plus four of the Santa Barbara Channel Islands.

Where are the traditional Chumash lands?

The Chumash once lived along 200 miles of southern California coastline. They also lived on four of the Santa Barbara Channel Islands. The names of these islands are Anacapa, San Miguel, Santa Rosa, and Santa Cruz. When the European explorers arrived, the Chumash lands covered about 7,000 square miles. By the late 1990s, the Chumash owned only one small reservation in Santa Ynez, California. It covers about 75 acres of land.

Islands off the southern California coastline were one home of the Chumash.

What has happened to the population?

In 1770, there were between 10,000 and 22,000 Chumash. In 1920, there were only 74 Chumash. In a 1990 population count by the U.S. Bureau of the Census, 3,114 people said they were Chumash.

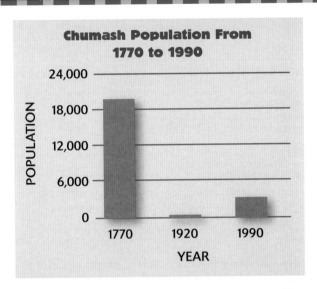

Origins and group ties

Scientists believe that the ancestors of the Chumash traveled across an ancient land bridge. Between twelve thousand and twenty-seven thousand years ago, this bridge joined Siberia to Alaska. The land bridge no longer exists.

There were at least six groups of Chumash. Five groups were named for the Catholic missions built in their territory. The largest group was called the Ynezeño. Almost nothing is known about the sixth group, the Interior Chumash.

Many Chumash today keep tribal traditions alive.

For thousands of years, the Chumash sailed up and down the California coast to fish. Their wooden boats were painted in bright colors. They traded with tribes in faraway places. The tribe was treated harshly by Spanish Catholic missionaries and Mexican and American settlers. Many thought the tribe had become extinct. Chumash descendents have quietly kept their culture alive. They want to keep their privacy and protect sacred artifacts from vandals and land developers.

The Chumash fished the waters of the Pacific Ocean. They also traveled great distances in boats to trade with other tribes.

HISTORY

Visitors from Spain

Chumash territory has been lived in for at least nine thousand years. By about A.D. 1000, the Chumash had taken control of lands that became present-day southern California. The Chumash were once one of the largest Native American groups in California. The tribe traded heavily with its neighbors. The Chumash traded acorns, shells, beads, and fish for animal skins, herbs, seeds, and nuts. They also traded soapstone, which is a soft stone that can be carved into pipes and bowls.

The early Chumash were hunter-gatherers. They had an organized political and economic system. The traditional ways of the Chumash did not interest the Spanish, Mexicans, or Americans

Soapstone was an item the Chumash traded up and down the southern California coast. They carved animals and other items out of the soft stone.

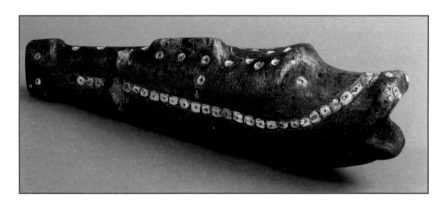

who invaded their lands. These newcomers never wrote about Chumash customs. It was a long time before people became interested in what Chumash society was like before the Europeans arrived. By then, there were few Chumash left who could remember the old ways.

The Chumash Indians first met European explorers in the 16th century. In 1542, Juan Rodríguez Cabrillo led a small fleet of Spanish ships along the Santa Barbara coast. Cabrillo was on a search for riches and a northwest passage through North America. In his travels, he met up with the Chumash. They were a friendly, peaceful people. The Chumash are said to be the first group of Native Californians ever encountered by Europeans.

Cabrillo claimed the area for Spain before he left. In 1602, Spanish explorer Sebastián Vizcaíno sailed through

This monument features a statue of explorer Juan Rodríguez Cabrillo, who claimed Chumash lands for Spain in 1542.

1869
Transcontinental railroad is completed

1917–1918
WWI fought in Europe

1929
Stock market crash begins the Great Depression

1941
Bombing at Pearl Harbor forces United States into WWII

1945
WWII ends

1950s
Reservations no longer controlled by federal government

1978
Chumash Indians agree to end their three-day protest at the site of an ancient burial ground

1989–1990
The National Museum of the American Indian Act and the Native American Grave Protection and Reparations Act bring about the return of burial remains to native tribes

Chumash waters. He named Santa Barbara Bay in honor of Saint Barbara's birthday as he looked for a port. For the next 160 years, the Chumash had no further visits from Europeans.

Spanish build missions to protect California

By the 16th century, Spanish explorers had claimed a vast amount of land in what is today the state of California. Over the next two hundred years, Russian and English explorers arrived in the area. To protect their claim to the territory, the Spanish began to build missions in 1769. The missions were part fort, part plantation, and part religious center. Spain expected the Indians there to help in this huge task. The Spanish wanted to make the natives more like Europeans. They tried to teach the Indians the Spanish language. Catholic priests, called padres, made the Indians build the missions without any pay. The priests also wanted to convert the natives to the Catholic religion.

In 1772, Spain built its first mission in Chumash territory at San Luis Obispo. In all, twenty-one missions were built in California. Five of them were built in Chumash territory. The missions became forced–labor camps for the Indians. The mission system came to an end more than sixty years later. By that time, the Chumash way of life had been destroyed.

Becoming "Mission Indians"

The Spanish brought farm animals such as cattle into Chumash territory. These animals trampled the local plant life and reduced the food supply. Game animals that once ate these plants became scarce. The Chumash economy was badly hurt. By 1824, all of the Channel Islands Chumash who had not been killed by Russian whalers became part of the

Native Americans were expected to learn to be more like Europeans at the Spanish missions. They were called "Mission Indians."

mission system. When some Chumash refused to join the missions, they were kidnapped by Spanish soldiers and forced to join. The Chumash and other tribes who belonged to the missions are often called "Mission Indians."

Spanish law said that Indians had to live near the missions once they were baptized into the Catholic faith. The newly baptized Chumash had to leave their villages. They lived in filthy, disease-ridden camps outside the missions. At the mission, they went to mass and had to work very hard without pay. They were trained to be carpenters, farmers, or any other job that the Spanish thought useful.

Chumash men, women, and children were often beaten and imprisoned. If they disobeyed the

Mission Indians, many of whom were Chumash, were expected to work hard without pay at the Spanish missions.

Converted Chumash were forced to live in homes near a mission. Pictured here is the ruin of such a dwelling.

missionaries' rules, they were sentenced to harsh physical labor.

Mexico takes over

In 1824, the Chumash decided to revolt. Indians from several missions rose up in protest. They took over La Purísima Mission for more than a month. They finally surrendered after an attack by Spanish troops. Many of the Chumash who led the rebellion were executed.

In 1823, the newly independent nation of Mexico gained control of present-day California. Ten years

Mission Purisima (pictured) was taken over by Chumash in the Great Chumash Revolt of 1824. The Spanish took back control and executed the rebellion's leaders.

later, the Mexican government took over the California missions. The Mission Indians were set free. Mexican officials promised to give land to the Indians. It was the same land where the Chumash had hunted and built villages for thousands of years. The Mexican government did not keep its promise. Instead, large numbers of Mexican settlers moved into California. They wanted the former mission lands for themselves.

The people are divided

From 1769 to 1832, nearly two-thirds of the Chumash died from illness and the harsh mission life. The survivors were no longer connected to their ancient villages and way of life. Some worked without pay for the Mexicans. Others moved to find jobs in Los Angeles and other new towns along the coast. Some went to the center part of California to find new homes among other tribes. Many became outlaws. They stole farm animals from Mexican cattle ranches. Some were killed in the attempt.

In 1848, the United States took California from Mexico. That same year, gold was discovered in the area. Americans moved in large numbers to California. The Spanish and the Mexicans had used the Indians as slaves. The Americans simply wanted

In 1849, many Americans moved to California to search for gold. They, as well as other settlers, did not want to share the land with the Native Americans.

the Indians out of their way. In only a few years, American settlers had killed thousands of California Natives, many of them Chumash. Many Indians died from the new illnesses that the whites brought to the area.

A few acres are set aside for the Chumash

In 1851, the U.S. government set up a reservation system in California. At first, the California reservations were created on military lands to protect Natives from the violence of other Californians. The government lands could not serve more than two thousand Indians. Most California Indians had to survive as best they could on their own.

A reservation was set aside for the Chumash in 1854. It quickly fell apart because the people who ran it were dishonest. Like other California Indians, the Chumash moved to far-off areas to hide from settlers. The violence against them continued. Some Chumash were murdered by white setters. Others were killed in army massacres.

In 1901, a small group of Chumash was given 75 acres near the former Santa Ynez Mission. The site became California's smallest reservation. It is called the Santa Ynez Chumash Reservation. There is not enough land on the reservation to support many people. Because there are no jobs there, most

Chumash can stay there for only a short time. Most live in small groups throughout their former territory.

American settlers continued to attack Native Americans in California, so the Chumash hid to escape the abuse. Some whites thought the whole tribe had died out. Although the Chumash tribe is a tiny fraction of its once great size, the group and its culture have survived.

In 1901, a small reservation for the Chumash was set up on 75 acres near Santa Ynez Mission (pictured).

Religion

The Chumash thought of the land and ocean in a spiritual way. They called the earth the World of the People.

The Chumash believed in three worlds: the Sky World, the World of the People (Earth), and the Lower World (where evil beings lived). According to Chumash tradition, animals were Earth's first creatures. When death appeared on Earth, some animals rose into the sky to escape it. These animals

turned into heavenly bodies such as the Sun, Moon, and the Evening Star.

The chief of the Sky People was Eagle. He held up the sky with his wings. If any of the Sky People became upset, terrible storms would rain down on the World of the People. The Chumash believed that when people died, they had to travel through the heavenly bodies to reach the afterworld.

One ritual of the Chumash religion was to take a drug called *toloache*. It was made from a plant called jimsonweed. The drug caused people to go into a trance and see visions. Chumash religious leaders were also astrologers. They could read signs in the stars of the nighttime sky.

The Spanish priests who ran the missions forced the Chumash to give up their traditional practices. When the mission system ended in the 1800s, some Chumash went back to their traditional religious practices . Many, however, kept the Christian belief in a supreme being. Although most modern-day Chumash say they are Catholic, few attend mass.

Government

Under the Indian Reorganization Act (IRA) of 1934, tribes were encouraged to form tribal governments. The Chumash formed a general council to govern the reservation. The council is made up of all members of the tribe age twenty-one and older.

Economy

Before the Spanish came, the Chumash gathered and traded for a living. The different groups of Chumash traded their local goods with each other. For example, the Chumash who lived on the islands collected shells. They traded their shells for grains and animal skins from the Chumash who lived on the mainland.

Workers belonged to organizations called guilds. Guild members set prices for their goods. Sometimes, villages held fairs. Guild members would set up booths at a marketplace. Customers from far away would travel to the market to buy and trade goods.

Channel Island Chumash used shells to purchase goods from Chumash who lived on the mainland.

DAILY LIFE

Families

Chumash families were large. A family was made up of a husband and wife, their married sons and their wives, their unmarried children, and other close relatives of the husband. Often, forty to seventy people lived together in the same house.

Buildings

Most Chumash built large, dome-shaped houses. Some were up to 50 feet wide. These homes were built in long neat rows separated by narrow streets. Shingles made of plants and grasses covered each

As many as seventy people could live in the large, round Chumash houses. A Chumash family included many relatives besides the parents and children.

home's wooden frame. In the center of each home was a fire to cook food. The smoke from the fire escaped through a hole in the ceiling. Sleeping areas were separated by grass mats hung from the ceiling.

Most villages had sweathouses. These houses or caverns were heated by steam. They were used for rituals to purify the body. Chumash sweathouses were built partly underground. They were entered through a hole in the roof.

The southern California heat kept the Chumash from wearing much clothing. They usually did not wear shoes.

Clothing

Because the weather where they lived was warm, the Chumash wore simple clothing. Men wore only a string around the waist. They hung tools and food from it. Sometimes, they wore an animal skin around their hips if the weather was cool. If it was very cold, they wore cloaks. These cloaks were also made of animal skins. Only the rich and powerful wore bear and other fur.

Women wore two aprons—a large one hung from the waist in back and a smaller one in front. The aprons were made of buckskin, shredded bark, or grass. A fringe of shells hung from the bottom edge. The people usually went barefoot. Moccasins were used only on special occasions.

Some Chumash males had pierced noses, and many had pierced ears. The ear holes were large enough to hold containers of tobacco. For special occasions, the people wore body paint.

Food

The coastal and island Chumash had plenty of food and water. Life was harder for the Chumash who lived in the rugged California interior. The women gathered food and the men hunted. Sometimes, widows became hunters to get food for their families.

The most important food in the Chumash diet was acorns. During the harvest season, people from several Chumash villages worked together to gather the acorns. Then, acorns were ground into flour. The

Acorns were stored in a building called a granary.

Chumash also ate nuts, wild seeds, and roots. The Chumash people hunted deer, elk, rabbits, squirrels, ducks, and geese. They fished in rivers and the ocean. From the ocean, they had fish, clams, mussels, crabs, and crayfish. Hunters in canoes harpooned seals, sea otters, and porpoises.

Education

Before the arrival of the Spanish, Chumash children probably learned as they watched their elders. During the mission period, Indian children were taught the basics of the Catholic religion. They also learned how to farm, weave, and make pottery. The Spanish thought these trades were useful. European

Mission Indians including the Chumash were instructed in the Catholic religion but were not taught to read. In California, it was illegal to teach Native Americans to read until the 1920s.

settlers did not want to teach the Chumash to read. They feared that educated Indians might become angered by the unjust mission system. In California, it was against the law to teach Indian children to read until the 1920s.

In the early 20th century, the U.S. government built a school on the reservation. It did not stay open for long. Most Chumash children spoke only broken English. They faced prejudice at the public schools at Santa Ynez near the reservation. By the mid-1990s, a little more than half of the reservation population had completed high school. The school dropout rate for the Chumash is high. Some Chumash drop out of school to work to help support their families.

Shamans healed people with charm stones and herbs.

Healing practices

The Spanish who first met the Chumash described them as healthy. Many Chumash lived to a very old age. The person who cured the sick was the shaman (pronounced *SHAH-mun* or *SHAY-mun*). Shaman is another word for medicine man. Shamans used herbs and charm stones to heal people. Charm stones were polished rocks believed to have great power. Shamans also used a special tube to blow or suck out an object that caused illness. (The object was

usually just a stone that the shaman had brought with him.) The shaman then sang and danced over the sick person.

Arts

The Chumash were fine artists. They are best known for their pictographs in caves. These brilliantly colored images of humans, animals, and abstract circles might have been part of a religious ritual.

The Chumash carved beautiful bowls and animal figures from a soft stone called soapstone. The Chumash wove twine through fiber baskets to make them watertight. Then, the baskets were dyed black.

The Chumash left behind finely painted pictographs.

CUSTOMS

Class system

Chumash society had an upper, middle, and lower class. Shamans and priest-astrologers belonged to the upper class. Members of the guild that made canoes were also part of the upper class. Skilled, healthy workers belonged to the middle class. The lower class was made up of people who lacked special skills or who were sick.

Festivals

Two of the most important festivals celebrated the autumn acorn harvest and the winter solstice. The winter solstice is the longest night of the year, when

Modern-day Chumash women attend a powwow.

winter begins. Other ceremonies honored animals. Men and women wore body paint for these festivals.

War and hunting rituals

The Chumash did not wage war often. When a conflict could not be avoided, they sometimes held a mock battle. The opponents dressed in full war costume. The two sides lined up to face each other. One member from each side took a turn and shot an arrow at the other side. When one person was killed, the battle was over.

Puberty

When Chumash girls neared puberty, they had to follow certain rules. One rule forbade them to eat meat and grease. To celebrate the start of puberty, both boys and girls took the drug *toloache*. It sent them into a trance, where they met their guardian spirits.

Marriage

Most Chumash men chose their brides from their own village or one nearby. A wealthy man might choose a bride from a faraway village. Except for the chief and his assistants, Chumash men had only one wife. After a wedding ceremony where everyone sang and danced, the couple moved into the home of the groom's family.

Jimsonweed was the source of *toalache*, a drug the Chumash used during rituals.

Birth

When a pregnant Chumash woman began to feel labor pains, she dug a pit in the ground. She would then lie down in the pit. The woman went through labor and delivery without physical help, but with a shaman present. After she gave birth, the mother broke her infant's nose bone because a flat nose was considered attractive. The child was named by the shaman. He looked to the stars for help when he picked a name.

A Chumash shaman would observe the stars for inspiration while he thought of the name for a newborn.

Death rituals

The Chumash were very respectful of the dead. Several mourners sat overnight with the body of a dead person. The body was then carried to the cemetery. Mourners gathered and smoked tobacco, sang, and cried. Then the body was buried face down. Sometimes a pole was placed on top of the grave. From it hung objects that had special meaning to the dead person. If the dead person was very important, the body might be burned along with the person's entire house. The Chumash still burn a dead person's possessions.

The Chumash work hard to preserve their cultural ways.

Current tribal issues

Efforts to keep the Chumash culture alive have faced many problems. The U.S. government recognizes only the Chumash who live on the reservation. The government will only give aid to federally recognized tribes. Because the Chumash reservation is on such a small piece of land, only fifty to one hundred people can live there at any one time. Off-reservation Chumash have formed groups to preserve their culture. They have not been successful in their attempts to get federal recognition.

The Chumash work hard to protect sacred sites from vandals and land developers. In the 1800s, Chumash cemeteries were raided. Many of the art objects found there were sold to museums and art collectors.

Notable people

Pacomio (José) Poqui (c. 1794–1844) was raised and trained as a carpenter at La Purísima Mission. He was unhappy with the way his people were treated by the Spanish. He helped to lead a group of two thousand Indians against the missionaries in an 1824 uprising. The Indians held the mission for about a month before they were forced to surrender.

F. L. Kitsepawit (c. 1804–1915) lived in the mission at Ventura as a young man. He was not able to speak his native language there. Later, like other Chumash, he lived in far-off areas. He worked as a ranch hand and carpenter. Toward the end of his life, he was contacted by the Smithsonian Institution. The museum wanted to know his memories of the Chumash culture before it had been upset by the Spanish and Americans. Kitsepawit was able to remember many things from his childhood. Because of him, some of the traditions, history, and language can be brought back to the Chumash people.

F.L. Kitsepawit helped preserve Chumash traditions and language by sharing his childhood memories with the Smithsonian Institution.

For more information

Duvall, Jill. *The Chumash.* Chicago: Childrens Press, 1991.

Gibson, Robert O. *The Chumash.* New York: Chelsea House, 1991.

Grant, Campbell. *Rock Paintings of the Chumash: A Study of a California Indian Culture.* 1965. Reprint, Santa Barbara, CA: Santa Barbara Museum of Natural History/EZ Nature Books, 1993.

Keyworth, C. L. *California Indians.* New York: Facts on File, 1991.

Glossary

Guilds associations of people who did similar work

Missions churches built in California by the Spanish in the 1700s

Pictographs drawings or paintings on rock walls

Reservation land set aside for Native Americans by the government

Shaman a Native American priest who used magic to heal people and see the future

Toloache a drug made from jimsonweed used to produce a trance or hypnotic state

Index